KEEP GOING CINEMA
PRESENTS

BREAK FREE!
HOOD EDITION

Breaking Free from the Mindset That's Keeping You Stuck

By ELISA GARCIA

"Keep Growing, Keep Going!"™

Scripture quotations are taken from the following translations:

Disclaimer:
This book is based on real-life experiences; however, certain names, details, and identifying characteristics have been changed to protect the privacy of individuals. Any resemblance to actual persons, living or dead, or actual events is either intentional (where permission has been granted) or coincidental.

This work is for informational and inspirational purposes only and does not constitute financial, legal, or professional advice. The author makes no guarantees regarding outcomes based on the application of the ideas presented. The author has made reasonable efforts to ensure that the portrayal of individuals is respectful and accurate to the best of their knowledge.

KEEP GOING CINEMA, LLC
keepgoingcinema.com
ISBN Paperback: 979-8-9959961-1-8
ISBN eBook: 979-8-9959961-0-1

DEDICATION

All the Glory to God! Helehn and Bella, my best friends sent from heaven, thank you for always supporting my crazy ideas, no matter what! I love you dearly!!! Ama, gracias por su apoyo siempre! Apa, gracias por ser un ejemplo de perseverancia. Los quiero.

CONTENTS

INTRO

There has to be more to life than this! right? I agree. Many years ago, that was my hope. I knew that I didn't want to live in a place destined for oppression, filled with poverty, crime, gang violence, murder and decided that I was going to figure a way out. **Decided**. That means that getting out the hood began in my mind. It took me 29 years, but I finally made it out! and I'm going to show you how.

If you don't know a word I use in this book, look it up! Words are powerful, full of meaning and hope. You are here because you are doing things in a new way, you want more for your life therefore to see a change you have to *make* a change.

Before you begin reading, answer this question. How do you see yourself right now in all areas of your life? Go deep. Use details. Be honest. Date it.

CHAPTER 1 CHOOSE WISELY

Growing up in South Central Los Angeles, California, the youngest of four, born seven years after my older sister, I witnessed many things. My two older brothers fell into the trap of joining a gang and years later gang violence would wreak havoc in our family. One of the benefits of having much older siblings was good music. I grew up listening to oldies, Brenton Wood, Big Jay McNeely, Zapp and Roger, West Coast rap and since my parents spoke Spanish only, Regional Mexican music was also part of my upbringing.

I began attending Locke High School and loved it. Although Centennial High was down the street from our home, my brother thought Locke High was a better option. This was the 2000's and hip-hop artists like Ashanti, J-Lo, Alicia Keys and Aaliyah were a strong influence in my style. I've always been interested in expressing my creativity through clothing. Music videos were my inspiration for arranging cute outfits for school and I always had a one-time use camera to take pictures; cell phones were rare. I would take my camera to Sav-On and wait a week for my pictures to develop, I know! Rare.

It's 2003, I was sick with the flu for three days. Friday morning I felt better and went to school, little did I know a few hours later my entire life would change profoundly. At the time, my brother and I weren't speaking, I don't recall the reason, but we were too proud to apologize to each other. This became one of my biggest regrets. Don't leave for tomorrow, what can be done today...it may be too late. The decisions you make today will impact your future, choose wisely.

....

MINDSET SHIFT 1

MAKE A WISE DECISION RIGHT NOW, IN WRITING. YOU ARE ONE DECISION FROM LIVING A NEW LIFE! HAVING HOPE IS PART ONE AND PART TWO IS TAKING ACTION CONSISTENTLY.

You are worthy, one of a kind and one **decision** away from living a new, full life. Keep Growing, Keep Glowing, Keep Going, Keep Pouring!™

"Then God said, "Let us make mankind in our image, in our likeness..."

Genesis 1:26 NIV

I ______________________________ (insert your name) DIVORCE MYSELF FROM THE HOOD, FROM A MINDSET OF LACK. THERE IS MORE FOR MY LIFE. GOD CREATED ME IN HIS IMAGE AND LIKENESS TO BE ABUNDANT, TO CREATE, AND TO LIVE A FULL LIFE.

Sign ___________________ Date _____________ **Read 100x's daily.**

....

Reflection & Alignment Notes:

CHAPTER 2 PRESSURE REFINES

Friday afternoon at school, I hear my name being called in the loud speaker. My sister and brother in law showed up unexpectedly. We walked to the front of the school and stopped for a moment, she looked at me and said our brother was shot. I didn't quite capture the meaning. I'm thinking, ok he got shot but he's alright? Right? My sister responded, "No, he's gone!" I released a mourning wail and painfully and inconsolably cried during the drive home, the crime scene. My brother and his friend were shot by rival gang members, in front of our home. That was the moment I realized, I never apologized to him and it was too late now. He's gone! and there was no way to make amends. Pride is like stepping into quicksand and refusing help while sinking, until it's too late. Don't wait until "He's gone!" Apologize today.

There was devastation in my home for a long time. My parents were distraught, my siblings in disbelief and me, at sixteen years old attending my brother's murder trial. I became responsible for keeping my family informed during the entire process, I rode the bus to the Compton courthouse and spent my days listening to endless evidence, objections and rebuttals. Keep this courthouse in mind because years later it would make an interesting connection to my life. "Guilty!" I heard, justice was served for my brother and his friend and a giant outcry followed by the defendant's family because at that moment, they too lost their sons— to the prison system.

....

MINDSET SHIFT 2

SHOW UP. EVEN WHEN IT'S INCONVENIENT, EVEN WHEN IT'S PAINFUL, EVEN WHEN PRESSURE IS HIGH. USE IT AS FUEL! THINK OF COAL, GRAPES AND OLIVES – WITHOUT THE PRESSURE THERE WOULDN'T BE DIAMONDS, WINE OR OIL.

Since you made it to Mindset Shift 2, Congratulations!!! on taking the first step!!!

"Not only so, but we also glory in our sufferings, because we know that suffering produces perseverance; perseverance, character; and character, hope."

Romans 5:3-4 NIV

....

Reflection & Alignment Notes:

CHAPTER 3 POSSIBILITIES

Since most of my mother's family lived in San Francisco, I had the opportunity to live in two completely different lifestyles. Most of the year, I lived in South Central Los Angeles, California "The Hood" and spent summers in San Francisco, California "The Bay".

In the Hood, I developed roots to persevere, an understanding for survival, a hunger for growth, which became resilience. I spend a lot of time alone and distracted by television which distorted my mind in many ways; creating a slowly destructive, numbing habit that silently formed obstacles in my path, and competed for my attention for many years into adulthood. When my siblings began having children at a young age, I had mini companions since most of them lived with us. I would dress them up with my clothes and we would have modeling photo sessions, we loved it!

The Bay represented a bigger picture, potential, alternatives, hope. I developed a work ethic and an interest for entrepreneurship. As a kid, I would charge my aunts by the minute for back massages, and they would pay! I worked helping my aunt clean beautiful, Victorian houses in downtown San Francisco. I had many cousins around my age that I was close to and we would see each other often for family gatherings and dinners. I was exposed to family-like activities and was fortunate to see more of the world by camping, going to the snow, picnics, theme parks, which allowed me to create different, beautiful childhood memories and subconsciously I became aware that there was more to life. I am grateful for the exposure to both. They were essential in shaping who I have become and it's a clear indication that being exposed to a change of scenery will alter your perspective about life.

....

MINDSET SHIFT 3

VISIT OTHER CITIES OUTSIDE YOUR OWN, OBSERVE HOW PEOPLE MOVE, LOOK AT THE POSSIBILITIES. GO TO THE CITY YOU WANT TO LIVE IN AND DO ACTIVITIES THAT YOU ALWAYS WANTED TO TRY. BREAKING FREE FROM THE HOOD BEGINS IN YOUR MIND, YOUR SURROUNDINGS DETERMINE YOUR PERSPECTIVE. WHY NOT YOU?

Because Abraham *believed* God, God gave Abraham land as far as his eyes could *see.*

> "All the land that you see I will give to you and your offspring forever."
>
> Genesis 13:15 NIV

....

Reflection & Alignment Notes:

CHAPTER 4 SOLID FOUNDATION

One day, my boyfriend came over to my house. My brother's friend stopped by asking for my brother, "He isn't home" I responded. For the following weeks this friend would continuously ask me out. I would reject and remind him that I had a boyfriend. He eventually won me over. One night, my brother, his family, this friend and I went to the movies. This friend sat next to me and attempted to hold my hand, I pulled my hand back and went to the bathroom to break up with my boyfriend. I was honest. I wasn't a cheater, growing up my Pops had two families and I witnessed how much hurt that caused my family, I despised cheating, and had my mind set on never allowing infidelity in my relationships. I returned to the theatre as an unattached young woman and the relationship with my "forever love" began. After high school, my plan was to go to college and build a career before having children. It is imperative to have a solid foundation about the vision for your life, otherwise it will drastically change and will be led by circumstance instead. Although going to college was my plan, I had many voids, neglect was one of them. Shortly after, my "forever love" declared his desire for me to become the mother of his children. I was honored and accepted gladly, I felt chosen. I longed to be greatly loved, cared for, wanted, needed and I desired a tight knit family. I subconsciously selected my "lifetime" partner based on what I lacked in my life. Had I had an understanding about my true identity, a solid foundation about the vision for my life, and not prematurely awakened desire, I could have spotted the red flags; false impressions, instabilities, continuously tall tales, deception, and inconsistencies. I became a teen mom at 17, and had my second child at 21, I loved being a mom. Before my children I had a self centered mindset, I now felt the responsibility and had the opportunity to become a good role model.

....

MINDSET SHIFT 4

WRITE OUT WHAT YOU ALWAYS ENVISIONED FOR YOUR LIFE. TAKE INVENTORY AND GET RID OF ALL DISTRACTIONS. YOU BECOME LIKE THE PEOPLE YOU SPEND THE MOST TIME WITH. IF YOU WANT TO CHANGE BUT THE PEOPLE CLOSE TO YOU DON'T, CUT THEM LOOSE OR THEY WILL DRAG YOU DOWN. FOCUS ON YOUR SKILLS & INTERESTS, THEY ARE NOT

A MISTAKE. YOU WERE CREATED WITH PURPOSE. UNDERSTAND YOUR TRUE IDENTITY, GOD CALLS YOU A MASTERPIECE!

"For we are God's masterpiece. He has created us anew in Christ Jesus, so we can do the good things he planned for us long ago."

Ephesians 2:10 NLT

....

Reflection & Alignment Notes:

CHAPTER 5 NOURISH YOUR MIND

About 10 years later my "forever love" left, after impregnating and marrying another woman while living in our home. I was devastated, the one fear I had came true. All I wanted was to have a tight knit family and now it was broken. After taking time to heal, I made a **decision** to give up my rental house, quit my job and move in with my Mom to focus on discovering my "passion". This was before I had a relationship with God but I remember telling God, "I'm ready, test me!" and He did! My brother and his family also lived there. My daughters and I stayed in my Mom's room, a back room where she didn't have a stove but a hot plate to cook our food, keep this in mind.

This set back was grounds for a comeback! I was feeling the pressure to lay a new foundation. I would drop off my children at school, workout, shower and head to the library to nourish and grow my mind by reading and listening to personal development and new ways to apply that information to transform my life.

I began seeing opportunities everywhere! This was a time in my life where I tried many odd jobs, the hustle was real for real! I was a salesperson for men's bespoke suits and our market was athletes. I wrapped gifts during the Christmas season, plated food at a private event, showed a couple their first dance for their wedding, did research for a government entity, and created a food stand, which I remember dearly.

This food stand was something else! A construction site began building near where I lived with my Mom. I saw an opportunity to supply a need for construction workers. I thought, since driving to buy food takes time away from their lunch break, I will sell home cooked meals near their site. My sales tactic? A wave. I began waving at the local truck drivers passing by, some drivers would stop to buy, some would stop out of confusion, but they stopped! After falling out with the person that was initially part of it, I communicated that I wanted to continue, and there was agreement. I took my tax refund and bought my own equipment. I used my Mom's hot plate to cook the food I sold, a hot plate! and recipes from YouTube, I was a one woman show, my Mom would help me load and unload. I created a welcoming atmosphere for my construction customers, a seating area in the shade and music playing as they arrived, they loved it, it was beautiful!

MINDSET SHIFT 5

GET A LIBRARY CARD, READ BOOKS, NOURISH YOUR MIND. ATTEND POWERFUL CONFERENCES THAT STRETCH YOU AND MAKE YOU UNCOMFORTABLE. LISTEN TO EFFECTIVE PERSONAL DEVELOPMENT CONTENT AND APPLY, APPLY, APPLY THOSE PRINCIPLES TO YOUR LIFE. SERVE OTHERS WITH LOVE.

"Do not conform to the pattern of this world, but be transformed by the renewing of your mind..."

Romans 12:2 NIV

Reflection & Alignment Notes:

CHAPTER 6 KEEP GOING!

A few months later a misunderstanding occurred and my brother kicked me out. Keep in mind that I didn't have a place to go, that's why I was living with my Mom so in the next few days, I arranged for my children to temporarily stay with their Dad and I was prepared to sleep in my car if needed. At the last minute, my sister finds out and offers me her house. Because I knew that if I gave up, my circumstances would never change, I diligently continued to grow my mind and applied to positions of opportunity. I was hired through a job agency to work for the Probation Department because of my criminal justice associate's degree. From that opportunity, I obtained a position at the District Attorney's office in the same courthouse that held my brother's murder trial. This is where my life made a significant change and God was starting to become more evident to me, even though He was there all along. After experiencing yet another traumatic experience with a deceiving man, I found myself heartbroken to the point that I felt death near. That relationship ended and I began working three jobs to make ends meet, and to pay the bills he left behind. I cried out to God, and He rescued me! I began reading the Bible, applying God's commands to my life and obeying the way He commands us to live. I enrolled back to school full time while now holding two jobs, working seven days a week and a year later, God blessed me with an outstanding opportunity that only He could have offered. God is so good! Not only did He blessed me, but He healed my heart, restored me, filled me with an unfailing love, joy and perfect peace. A love that I was unaware of but desperately needed, a joy that I thought I would never feel again, and a peace that I still feel today. He blesses those who walk in His ways. He is a just God who vindicates you, and repays all the evil done against you, in His perfect timing.

....

<u>MINDSET SHIFT 6</u>

SURRENDER AND SUBMIT TO GOD.

EVERY DAY and MOMENT of your life has already been planned. You are here to **fulfill** what was already written about you! Doesn't it make sense to partner up with the One who wrote the plan? As a bonus, know this: God thinks about you *more* than the grains of sand. You are not alone. He sees you!

"You saw me before I was born. Every day of my life was recorded in your book. Every moment was laid out before a single day had passed.

How precious are your thoughts about me, O God. They cannot be numbered! I can't even count them; they outnumber the grains of sand! And when I wake up, you are still with me!"

Psalm 139:16-18 NLT

Reflection & Alignment Notes:

CHAPTER 7 THE WAY

If I told you there is a way in which every **decision** you make would prosper, would you be interested in knowing? The way is Jesus. It doesn't have to take you 36 years like it did for me. Read the Bible. Begin living as God commands and watch your life shift faster than the 36 years that it took me to form an intimate relationship with God. Before God, I was trying to do it all on my own, my way and in my own understanding. Once I surrendered, accepted Jesus, and joined God's winning team, applied His ways to my life and obeyed His commands, He completely transformed my life in two years! 2!!! 2!!! 2!!!

You will surely experience challenges along the way, the difference is, you will have the protection and trust in the solid foundation of The Almighty God, which once you accept Jesus Christ, you will never be alone again.

"Do not fear, for I am with you; Do not be afraid, for I am your God. I will strengthen you, I will also help you, I will also uphold you with My righteous right hand."

Isaiah 41:10 NASB20

ACCEPT JESUS. SAY THIS PRAYER.

Father, I admit that I am a sinner. I believe that Jesus Christ was crucified, buried and resurrected on the third day, for my **salvation** which includes; the forgiveness of my sins, my complete inner and physical healing, deliverance from all bondage and captivity, prosperity, and eternal life. Lord Jesus, I confess and accept you as my Lord and Savior, I surrender and submit every area of my life to you. In Jesus Name, Amen.

"If you declare with your mouth, "Jesus is Lord," and believe in your heart that God raised him from the dead, you will be saved."

Romans 10:9 NIV

How do you **see** yourself NOW?

BREAK FREE! START NOW.

@KGCBREAKFREEHOODEDITION

Scan to start your 7 Day Identity Reset
or go to
keepgoingcinema.com

Identity frames what you believe possible.
You didn't read this book by accident.
If you go back to the same patterns, nothing changes. Everybody pays.
You either pay to learn or you pay for not knowing.
You are capable of more!

START NOW. BREAK FREE!

ABOUT ELISA GARCIA

Elisa Garcia is a woman of God. After living for herself for 36 years, through a painful experience she discovered the love of God and a new way of living. During a five hour flight returning from a powerful conference in Miami, Florida, Elisa wrote this book 30,000 feet in the air before landing in Los Angeles, California. This book was born from a desire to build others up by sharing true life experiences and what she has learned through trials, tribulations and transformation. One of the greatest principles she applied throughout her life was not giving up! That's how Keep Going Cinema™ was born, a movement to encourage others to persevere, embrace mindset transformation simultaneously serving as a reminder to herself. Life is a movie filled with mountains (highs) and valleys (lows), learn, adapt, adjust and Keep Going! Break Free! Start now.

@KGCBREAKFREEHOODEDITION

Every ACTION you take in the PRESENT is BASED on something you BELIEVE about the future.
Every ACTION you **DON'T** take in the PRESENT is BASED on something you BELIEVE about the future. Both are true. Pick one. Date it, write about it.

You believe. The question is, *what* do you believe in? Make a Decision. Commit Consistently. Execute. Why not you? Date it, write about it.

Keep Going!

"Keep Growing, Keep Going!"™

Made in the USA
Coppell, TX
09 June 2026

79280678R10015